STARTING
A
SCHOOL GARDEN

by
David Gale

STARTING A SCHOOL GARDEN
© David Gale 1987
ISBN 1-85116-800-1

First Published 1987 by School Garden Company,
P.O. Box 49,
Spalding,
Lincs. PE11 1NZ.
Telephone 0775-69518

David Gale is the Head Teacher of a primary school in Lincolnshire.

"The countryside is a very good place for finding problems, but somewhere that can be visited regularly and very frequently will be required when children wish to set up experiments designed to solve them."
(Using the Environment — Unit 4, 1975 Schools Council/Macdonald)

Printed by Abbey Printers Ltd., High Street, Spalding, Lincolnshire.

Contents

Illustrations

1
Introduction

The term **school garden** can be interpreted in a number of ways. It might include a woodland area, a pond, a wild patch, a play area and a cultivated plot. Each school has a different site. For some it will be easy to provide a **school garden**. Others will face real difficulties. Schools will have their own reasons for using their grounds in varying ways (see Fig. 1).

The purpose of this book is to help those concerning themselves with the provision of a small cultivated area, including perhaps a wild patch. Features such as ponds and play areas are excellent, but these are beyond the scope of this particular book. The aim here is to support you on your way to successful cultivation on a small scale and to provide ideas for practical activities and extension work so that your school garden is a worthwhile addition to the school for many years to come.

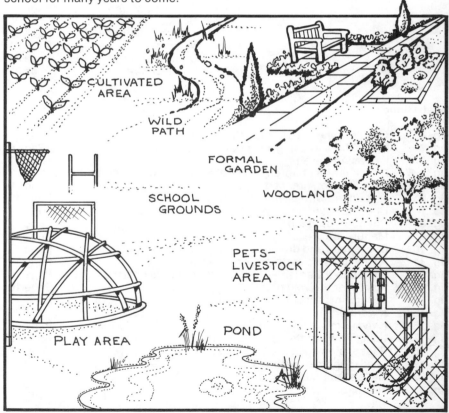

Fig. 1 — possible ways to develop the school grounds.

2
Why Have a Cultivated Garden Area?

Some of the most meaningful work produced in school results when children are fully involved. Participation is of fundamental importance. Discussion skills, problem solving, and investigative thinking are more easily encouraged when the work is seen to have purpose and relevance. The development and use of a cultivated garden area can be an interesting and rewarding class project. "Growing plants" is not seen as an end in itself. The aim is to use the area as a basis for experimentation and investigation.

"At the primary stage environmental education is seen as involving pupils in personal experience of the environment by direct exploration . . . . . Such environments will involve school gardens . . . . . Teachers are expected to use these experiences to develop language, numeracy, scientific methods of enquiry, aesthetic appreciation and creative expression."
(extract from "A statement of aims for the formal education service" — National Association for Environmental Education 1976).

There is clearly great value in working beyond the classroom, but fieldwork is not always easy to encourage. There may be difficulties in meeting the needs for supervision, or providing the necessary finances. However, we can profitably use the near environment. We can take the classroom *just beyond* the school wall and, equally, we can bring the 'just beyond' inside the room. The school's cultivated area should be a source of valuable experimentation. It can give rise to both short and long term investigations.

The cultivation of plants will give the children first hand experience of a "risk" business. There will be fascination and frustration because of the somewhat unpredictable outcomes. There will be a constantly changing emphasis. The children will be involved in making contrasts and comparisons, making decisions and testing out ideas. They will sort, classify, observe and record.

Visits can be made to farms, allotments, market gardens and wildflower areas to show the children examples of plants and their cultivation on a wider scale.

A cultivated area can lead children to appreciate plants and living creatures. Working with plants and small creatures should assist the children in developing a caring attitude towards the countryside in general. Hopefully it will contribute to the formation of an overall environmental concern.

There may be lasting benefits that some of the children will take on into their leisure activities either now or later, such as an interest in gardening, working with their hands and the flavour of the outdoor life. The whole exercise should be an enjoyable and worthwhile experience.

3
Making a Start on a Cultivated Garden Area

First of all, we must be clear what our cultivated area is for. What are we aiming to achieve? Will the children work in groups — each needing its own plot? Is the design of our garden related to the intended learning? Always keep in mind that we are talking about a learning resource. Remember that activities for the children should be meaningful and pleasurable.

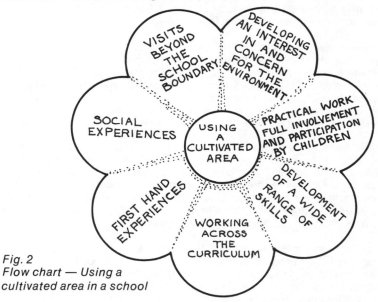

Fig. 2
Flow chart — Using a
cultivated area in a school

So we want the **smallest** plot which will enable the children to carry out the planned learning. Let the children do scale plans of likely areas on squared paper. If possible, plan for contrasting sites to allow for comparison of results. Alternatively, use containers for this purpose. Make sure your garden design takes into account the need to avoid too much digging. Relate the design to the work-load required (for children and teachers!) and to the likely maintenance needed to keep the area tidy and productive.

Your LEA groundsmen may have valuable ideas to contribute, both on the design and size of your area, and on minimising any extra maintenance work which the new area will demand of them. Time spent on such discussions at the planning stage may well limit any friction. (A number of schools know from experience that a school garden area is much easier to operate where the ground staff are interested and co-operative.) Don't plan for your ground staff to be actively involved in looking after the school garden area, as their very limited hours will probably not permit this.

4
Choosing a Site

Survey the school grounds and discuss the choice of site with the children. Look for a spot not overshadowed by trees or too close to a hedge as the roots will take the soil nutrients. Avoid too much shade from school buildings and stay away from areas where children play. Consider the prevailing wind direction and make sure your site is not exposed. The ideal site will have a sunny, reasonably sheltered position which is level or perhaps just on a slight slope. Check that the site is well drained. Another point worth considering is easy access to water as children will appreciate not having to carry heavy watering cans over any great distance.

Before settling on your site, try to get all the staff — including Head and Caretaker — involved in the discussions. Consider any problems of access (is the site close to an existing path?) and safety (does the Fire Brigade need to cross your site on its way to the school kitchens?) Check for dual-use (does the annual School Fair use the chosen plot?) and see that the various tools and other equipment can be stored somewhere close at hand. If possible, ensure the site will be visible from some parts of the school — "hidden" gardens can become forgotten eyesores — but not so close to a classroom that the garden might become a distraction.

If your school is on a windy, exposed site, then consider a hedge or a fence to give some protection. *Leylandii* is a fast growing evergreen hedge, but it will grow very tall if not clipped. *Beech, hornbeam* and *hazel* are good deciduous choices. Make sure that any hedge is not planted too close to the garden plots, as the roots will invade. Solid fences are not a good idea because of the turbulence. A hurdle fence or a simple wooden slat fence are reasonable alternatives.

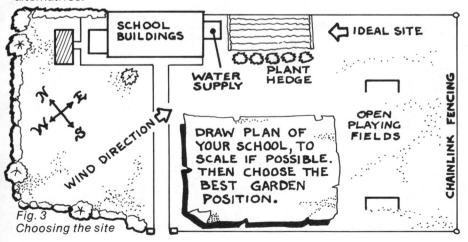

Fig. 3
Choosing the site

Fig. 4
Checklist for Children — Have you thought of everything?

5
Preparing the Site

Once you have chosen your site, preparation can begin. First you need to decide on the form your cultivated area is to take. Talk to your class about this and bear in mind the number of children involved as this will dictate overall dimensions and the number of plots necessary.

The following ideas may guide your deliberations and help you reach a conclusion as to the preferred design. You and your children may well be able to improve on the suggestions and in any case you have to work within the limitations of your own school grounds, and financial constraints.

Let's look at a simple approach to begin with. You could dig small plots out of a grass area similar to those shown in Fig. 5, having first decided how to go about the task. The small plot sizes mean that children can keep them weeded and look after their plants without spending too long, and also that access is easy without much need to walk on the soil areas themselves. Small groups might be given responsibility for each of the plots.

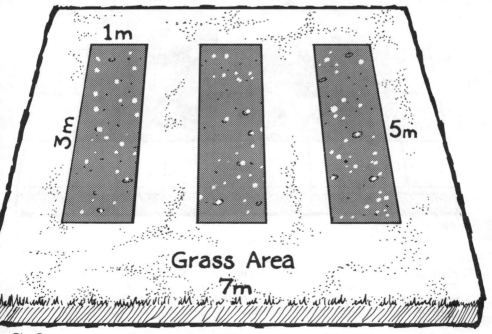

Fig. 5
Plot 5m x 7m; 3 plots of 1m x 3m surrounded by grass

Obviously there are variations as to the actual layout of the plots. The children can use a simple line and sighting post technique to measure out the individual plots. A design like this provides for easy access to plots but the surrounding grass is likely to wear and will often be wet. The edges will need cutting if each plot is to be kept tidy. The children will need to have wellington boots to hand. However, this is a cheap and easy way to get going on some cultivation and is well within the scope of many schools.

A development on this idea is to use small paving stones to edge the plots as this will save on maintenance and wear and tear. Fig. 6 is an example of this.

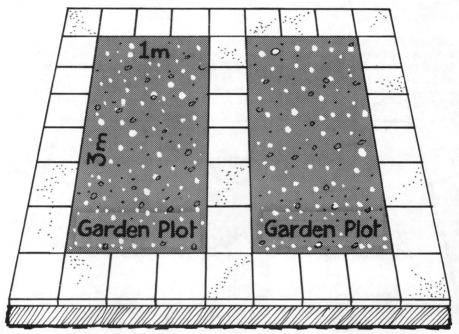

Fig. 6
Plot edged with paving stones.

A slightly more sophisticated approach uses the chequerboard garden idea. Plan a series of small plots — perhaps only 60cm x 60cm — set out in a chess-board fashion using paving stones. Let the children present possible designs to their classmates stating advantages and disadvantages. Emphasise again that designs must take into account the number of children to be involved. No more than four to a plot is suggested. Figures 7 and 8 show examples of chequerboard garden designs.

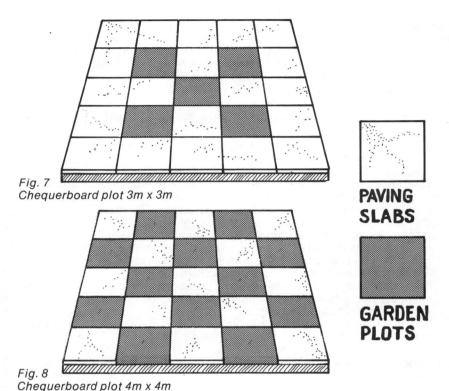

Fig. 7
Chequerboard plot 3m x 3m

Fig. 8
Chequerboard plot 4m x 4m

**PAVING
SLABS**

**GARDEN
PLOTS**

Garden designs like these minimise the digging necessary. Weeds are easy to control and general maintenance presents little problem. The gardens have the real benefit of looking attractive. Children have easy access to each individual plot, and there should only be a limited need for wellington boots. If the whole garden is set in the general grass area, then the gangmowers can cut right up to the paving stones — providing they are set nearly flush with the ground. Obviously the laying of paving stones could be a source of danger for the children so enlist help if possible from parents and other adults.

The purchase of paving stones might present a problem. Try the L.E.A. first. Justify the project as part of your curriculum development work and enlist the interest of your local inspector/adviser for Environmental Studies. If you can't get all the money, offer to go half and use PTA funds (assuming you have some!) You might want to ask at your local garden centre for help towards this. Tell them the local newspaper will be asked to do an article on your cultivated area and this should give publicity for their centre. They may donate the paving stones or help substantially towards their cost.

Before constructing the garden it is advisable to autumn dig the whole area to loosen the sub-soil. Lay the slabs the following spring on level sand or fine soil. Set the slabs to be a little 'proud' of the soil level in the working plots as this will prevent soil wash. Around the edges of the plot, the slabs should be slightly above the level of the surrounding grass. Fill in any gaps with soil, then firm and level. Sow a little grass seed. The gaps will soon merge back into the grassed area, making mowing easier.

Whatever type of garden you choose, good soil preparation will pay dividends, so:-

1.   Autumn dig to loosen and turn the soil. Let frost action break up the soil and make it crumbly.
2.   This in turn will improve drainage and allow the soil to warm.
3.   Thoroughly get rid of all weeds either by careful digging and removal or by using a weedkiller (a job for an adult). Clearly this raises a key issue on a wider scale, i.e. the general use of herbicides. Discuss this with the children, and emphasise safe use of any chemicals.
4.   Be careful when digging not to go too deep as the top soil should remain on top and not be lost. (Children can check the depth of top soil on your particular site and compare this with other local gardens etc.)
5.   Rake and prepare a fine tilth, say around 8cm deep.
6.   Previously well used soil will need improving by the use of fertiliser or manure. A local farmer may be kind enough to provide a load, and to talk with the children about his farm.
7.   If your soil is too sandy, then add manure. If it is heavy clay it will pay you to add coarse sand or very fine gravel, and mix it in well. Then add some manure.

Note:- most *wild* flowers prefer quite poor soil, with no fertilisers or manure added.

Manure is taken to mean such things as rotted horse or cow dung, spent mushroom compost and waste from deep litter chicken houses. They all contain some plant nutrients and add bulk to the soil, improving drainage and water holding capacity. They are termed *organic* materials since they are derived from living sources.

Fig. 9
Manure is . . . .

Fertilisers are sometimes termed *inorganic* or artificial since they are often pure chemicals mined from the earth. e.g. sulphate of potash (potassium sulphate). They are clean to use and a little goes a long way. Some fertilisers are organic in nature. They come from living things, but are such a concentrated source of mineral salts that they act in a similar way to inorganic fertilisers, e.g. bone meal.

Plants do of course require certain minerals for healthy growth. They take these in as food through their roots. The main minerals required are nitrogen, phosphates and potash. Manures and fertilisers contain such nutrients. Older children may be able to discuss the merits of organic fertilisers as against the inorganic. As a matter of expedience and convenience, most amateur gardeners might want to use a balanced proprietary inorganic fertiliser. The choice is yours.

If it is impossible to use a chequerboard garden or equivalent, then a substitute might be the use of **containers.** They have the advantage of being mobile, but they are prone to getting waterlogged if no proper drainage is provided. Conversely, they quickly dry out if drainage is good, so careful attention is needed in this respect. Small pots are the worst as they are easily kicked over or blown away. A good tip here is to use clay pots and a ''heavy'' potting compost (available from garden centres).

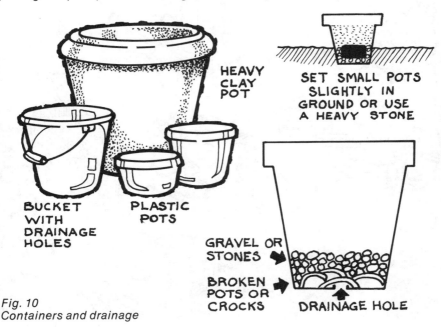

HEAVY CLAY POT

SET SMALL POTS SLIGHTLY IN GROUND OR USE A HEAVY STONE

BUCKET WITH DRAINAGE HOLES

PLASTIC POTS

GRAVEL OR STONES

BROKEN POTS OR CROCKS

DRAINAGE HOLE

Fig. 10
Containers and drainage

6
Sowing the Seeds

Sowing depends on several factors, including how many of each seed you have, and what investigations you wish the children to carry out. Sowing might be in drills (rows) or singly. The depth to plant will be according to the size of each seed variety. Bear in mind that some seeds do take a long time to germinate. If your seeds are in packets, then as a general rule, you should follow the instructions provided. Seeds will need careful watering and protection from birds. Keeping the birds away would be a good problem solving exercise for the children.

Use wildflowers, grasses, cereals and vegetables. Consider some simple seed experiments: try sowing thickly and thinly; in close rows and wider apart; in clumps and singly; deep and shallow; in different light and wind conditions on various parts of the plot. Numbered plastic markers and good recording by the children should yield some useful results!

Fig. 11
A very down to earth project

7
A Wild Patch in the School Grounds

So far we have concentrated on the provision of a formal cultivated area for use as a curriculum resource. You may also want to develop a wild patch as a less organised resource. Such an area would aim to encourage wildlife to come into the school grounds. There has been a real loss of hedgerow and meadow in the recent past and your own wild patch will be a contribution towards replacement. Ground plants, grasses and hedgerows will provide cover and food for many creatures, especially as the wild patch matures. A nature trail could be designed and there will be opportunities for outdoor work. Unlike a cultivated area, your wild patch can be rather large if you wish, giving plenty of room for different plants and habitats.

When developing your wild patch do remember that the law severely limits the collection of plants, including some weeds. This is a valuable area for class discussion. Further information is available from conservation bodies — see the **Appendix** for addresses.

Give careful thought to the siting of your wild patch. If allowed to grow naturally, it will **not** be a tidy garden and neighbours might not appreciate this! Weeds and wild flowers should not be allowed to seed into near-by gardens. The school ground staff should know about your project; try to get their co-operation. If might even be necessary to 'hide' your patch. This is discussed later.

Obviously if you have a cultivated area and a wild patch, they are best kept apart to avoid encroachment. You can start by just leaving an area to go wild. Decide on the best site, and don't cut the grass at all. Let the grasses and weeds establish themselves, and then wild flowers can be added by sowing seeds or by planting seedlings you have grown, perhaps on the classroom windowsill.

A more thorough approach is to choose a reasonably level piece of land, and remove the existing vegetation. This is best done by using weedkiller. Dig the ground well, making sure the soil is well broken to allow air and water in. Continue to keep weeds away at this stage. In the spring, start planting up. Put in grasses first, eg. bents and fescues. When the grass reaches about 8cm it can be cut. Now you should have a simple grass meadow and wild flower seed can be added. Try *cowslips, cornflowers, red campion, scabious, oxeye, daisy, harebell* — the choice is wide. Some seed companies sell excellent **grass and flower seed mixtures** which are selected for particular soil types. These might provide an ideal start for your new wild area. (Details of all these seeds are to be found in the **School Garden Company** catalogue — see **Appendix** for address.)

Fig. 12
The School Garden — Skills and Concepts chart

ENVIRONMEN

sorting, classi
testing, comp
differences, te
predicting out
experiments,
through obser
generalisation
of equipment.

LANGUAGE

discussion, decision-making, use of reference material, skimming, scanning, index, contents, note-making, written prose and poetry, descriptive work from observation, recording experiments.

The S
S

ART/CRAFT

observation and recording
observations using pencil, ink, pastel, paint, modelling e.g. clay.
looking at texture, colour, shape, pattern.
aesthelic appreciation, display skills.

SOCIAL

working in pa
give and take
for surroundi
countryside.

KEY CONCEPTS

1. Interdependence of living and non-living things
2. Cause and effect
3. The idea of change

Fig. 7

DIES

ontrol
ilarities and
otheses,
vising
ee pattern
king
   solving, use

MATHS
measuring, estimating, costing, using
equipment, making and interpreting
graphs, pattern, symmetry.

rden:

rt

MUSIC/MOVEMENT
movement themes involving the use
of space, working in co-operative
situation.
creative music making - using
instruments, making simple instruments, singing.

- sharing,
esponsibility
  for the

4.   The concept of growth
5.   Time
6.   The influence of man on nature
     and vice versa

When the flowers have gone to seed in the autumn the whole area should be cut, with the mower set high. Large stones, bark, tree stumps, logs and so on can then be added to make homes for mini beasts. Don't attempt to weed the patch. Remember that weeds are just successful wild plants. They may be a nuisance in the garden at home but they will provide a valuable learning source in your wild patch. They are persistent and spread very easily. They cost nothing, and are usually quite easy to identify.

A natural balance of the various species will gradually emerge — over several years — on your patch, and the relative success of the different plant types (introduced by you or by a number of natural means) can make an interesting long-term study.

As well as grasses, weeds, and wild flowers, you will find a **hedge** most useful. It can be a valuable screen for your area if you want to prevent neighbours from seeing or worrying about weeds and so on. A hedge will also assist the groundsman by defining the wild area and prevent children at play from running on to the area. Useful hedging plants will include *hawthorn, beech, privet, berberis, forsythia* and *leylandii*. The hedge should be dense and up to 1.5m high. Plants should be put in some 50 or 60cms apart. Trim the hedge back in the autumn but allow one or two bushes to grow into small trees. Take care with *privet* as it is a poisonous plant. For a wild area, a mixed hedge will provide a more varied habitat than a single-species hedge, even though the appearance will be less neat.

To attract **birds**, use *hawthorn, snowberry, privet, berberis* and *honeysuckle*. Also plant *nettles, knapweed* and *thistles,* as the birds will go for the seeds. Encourage **insects** for the birds by having stones, rocks and wood lying in the patch. Let the children design nest boxes and bird tables. Use this opportunity to teach them about not damaging or disturbing birds' nests and eggs.

To attract **butterflies**, plant *buddleia, honeysuckle, thrift, primroses, cornflowers, nettles* and *grasses*. The *nettles* will need periodic cutting back and shrubs will require pruning.

Bees will be drawn by *nasturtiums, teasels, cornflowers, creeping thyme, foxgloves* and *St John's wort*. A shrub like *dogwood* makes an interesting addition because of its attractive red or yellow bark.

The whole idea of a wild patch can be extended by looking at and developing specific plant communities, eg. heathland or marshland. There may be a suitable wild habitat close enough to visit, and a comparison of this with your school's wild area can be a good basis for interesting work.

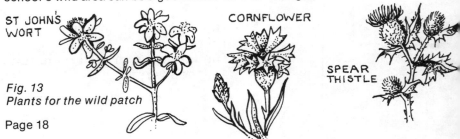

ST JOHN'S WORT   CORNFLOWER   SPEAR THISTLE

Fig. 13
Plants for the wild patch

8
Experiments and Investigations

"As with environmental education at all levels, the greatest impact is likely to be made with an investigatory approach using simple equipment which offers an extension to the senses."
(Project Environment — Education for the Environment — Longman Schools Council 1974).

Now we have a cultivated area planned and a wild patch on the way, let's see how we can use it for experimentation and investigation. The following suggestions are starters for teachers and children. They are presented in the form of notes for children, and will of course need to be expanded by the teacher before use.

They may lead children into devising their own experiments. Certainly the list is not exhaustive but the ideas will help the children discover many of the properties of soil and plants. Hopefully the children will also develop a positive attitude towards living things and a sense of personal responsibility.

Fig. 12 is intended to give teachers an indication of the skills covered during work on the garden and wild patch.

Experiments and investigations with soil

Collect different soil samples. Compare for odour, moisture, texture, size of particles, wet and dry characteristics, materials present, e.g. insects, plants. Use small plastic bags for samples.

Try to find samples of different soil types, e.g. sand, clay, loam. Set up an experiment to test respective drainage qualities. Consider the implications for gardeners and farmers. Find out all you can about the similarities and differences of clay, sand, silt, peat and loam.

Discover what soil contains by mixing some soil and water in a jar/container. Shake well and allow to settle. Identify the resultant layers. Why has the soil settled in this way? See fig. 14. Repeat this using different soil types. Compare and contrast the results. Can you now say what soil is?

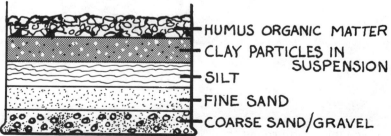

Fig. 14
Separating out soil constituents

Dig out a soil cube with sides of about 25 to 30cm. Chop the cube into three parts: ground level and above, the top 10cm of soil, and the lower 10cm. Investigate each layer for animal life. Make your recordings pictorially. Observe, sort, classify. Study some of the creatures in more detail. Are they insects? What is an insect? Return creatures to the environment they came from. You can do a similar investigation into the plant life and stones found in your soil block.

Use a **wormery** to discover how earthworms affect the soil. You need several different layers of soil. Something like this will suffice (Fig. 15). Lay some worms on the top layer of soil and record what happens.

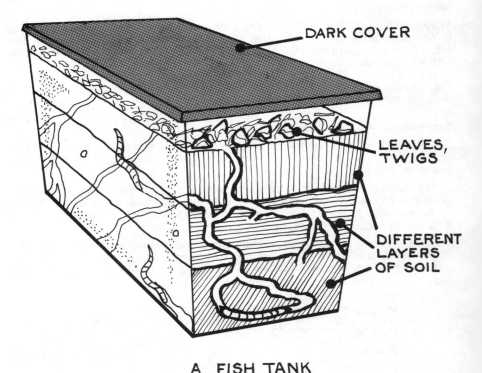

DARK COVER

LEAVES, TWIGS

DIFFERENT LAYERS OF SOIL

A FISH TANK

Fig. 15
A wormery

Do you think earthworms are useful creatures in the garden or are they pests? Say how they help the gardener.

Bring in a soil sample, enough to make a good layer in a small tank or plastic container (Fig. 16). Make a **vivarium** so you can study the creatures in your sample. Always treat creatures with care, and return them to their natural surroundings when your study has finished. Do the creatures live in or on the soil? Do some of them seem to live in both?

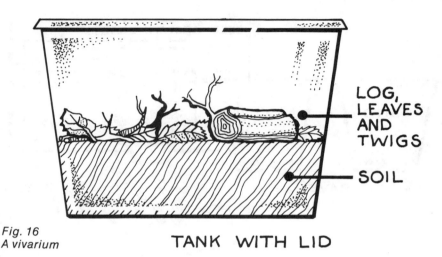

LOG,
LEAVES
AND
TWIGS

SOIL

Fig. 16
A vivarium   **TANK WITH LID**

Investigate the effect of soil colour on soil temperature by adding white sand and black coal dust to different samples of top soil. Put a 1cm layer on. Position an electronic thermometer two or three centimetres down. Record the temperature on a sunny day and on a dull day. Compare and discuss the results.

Look into the acid/alkaline qualities of the soil. Use a soil indicator solution. Red = acid, green = neutral, blue = alkaline. Use litmus paper pressed into a damp paste of soil. If it turns red, it indicates acid. If blue, it is an alkaline soil.

Try adding some lime to the soil specimen. How does this affect the acidity/ alkalinity? (Older children could use a soil testing kit to look at pH values etc.)

Make your own **Indicator Solution:**
Chop up some fresh red cabbage or fresh beetroot. Boil in 100ml water. Cool, then filter the solution into a separate container. Boil again until the solution has reduced to about half its original volume. This is your "red cabbage" indicator solution. Use as for the indicator solution (see above). Alternatively, soak a filter paper or small piece of white blotting paper in your indicator solution. Then let the paper dry out, and cut it into test strips. The colour changes are different . . . . what are they?

Grow seeds in sand and in soil. Make sure there are holes in the bottom of the flower pots (see Fig. 17). Water the seeds and cover with a polythene bag (make the safety point ref. polythene bags) and leave for up to ten days. Compare the rates of growth, the quality of the plants. Make a graph to show the growth rates. Try to grow some seeds using cotton wool and blotting paper as soil substitutes and make comparisons of the results.

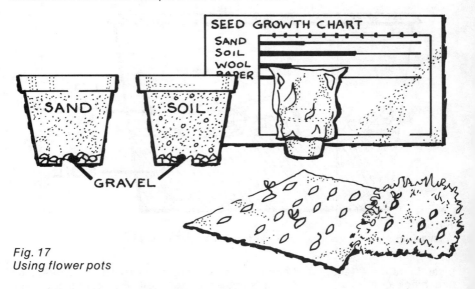

Fig. 17
Using flower pots

Experiments and Investigations with plants

Grow some seeds in an open plot and some in a mini greenhouse made by using black polythene. Try it with different seeds. Compare the results and consider the need for light by plants. (Creating the polythene greenhouse might be a useful design and problem-solving task for some of the children.)

Discover the influence of depth on sowing seeds. Put seeds in at different depths and record what happens. Do seeds need air to help them germinate?

Grow similar seeds in your plot and in a contrasting soil. Compare and discuss the results.

Plant out some seeds in quantity in two plots. As they grow, thin out one plot, but not the other. Is there any effect on the end results?

Leave a plot untended after some weeds have been planted. Compare this with a properly tended plot. Does the amount of tending affect the results?

Starting a School Garden   *Experiments*

Investigate the effect of heat on germination. Develop the black and white soil ideas in the soil experiments section: try similar trays of seeds, but one kept warm and one cool.

Grow some seeds in a fine soil. Are the results the same? Compare and discuss.

Can plant growth be improved by the use of fertilisers and manures? Devise experiments to test out this idea. (Safety — control the range and use of chemicals.)

Set up trials to discover the importance of water to growing plants. Remember it may rain and spoil your experiments! Do a similar exercise indoors.

What happens if you plant a seed upside down? Do shoots grow upwards and roots downwards no matter how the seed is planted? Test this out.

Investigate seeds closely. Get a large seed for this, e.g. broad bean, and carefully cut it open. Use a magnifier or microscope. What do you find? Use reference books to help you find out more about the inside of a seed.

Look at the different root systems and find out how they take in water. Compare different root systems for strength, depth of penetration into the soil, and spread.

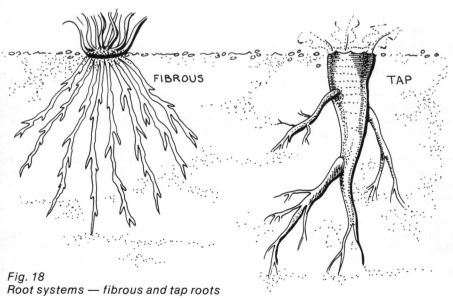

Fig. 18
Root systems — fibrous and tap roots

Study the work of a stem. Place the plant stem in a jam jar with coloured water in it (ink will do). Leave for a day, and then cut the stem in half along its length. What do you notice? What do you think has happened? Look at some different plants — can you find examples of different types of stems? Explore this idea.

Can parts of a plant grow again? Try a root, a stem, a leaf. Put into water first — if roots develop then transfer to a pot of good soil. Weeds are good for this experiment, e.g. *groundsel* and *dandelion.* Record your results pictorially and discuss your findings.

Stand a plant in a narrow bottle half full of water. Gently pour in a thin layer of cooking oil to 'seal' the surface. Mark the water level on the bottle. Leave on a window sill for a couple of days. Observe what happens to the water level. Where has the water gone? Does this tell you anything about the function of the stem? Why did we 'seal' the surface with oil?

Take a leafy plant. Put a plastic bag firmly over the plant. Observe and record what happens. Where does the moisture come from?

Place a plant in the dark for a few days. Note the difference to a 'control' plant kept in the light.

Crush a leaf (*nettles* are good) and place in clear methylated spirits. Note the green solution. What is it? Investigate chlorophyll.

Study the seeds of plants in your pots. Can you discover how they are dispersed? Investigate seed dispersal — wind, water, explosion, by creatures. Are seeds dispersed in any other way? Use reference books to help you find out.

Plants from the soil stuck to your wellington boots? Try it — who knows what might happen? First bake some soil to kill existing seeds. Then scrape the mud from your boots onto this soil, water it and cover with polythene. Leave in a warm place and check every day. Keep a record. Does anything grow? How has this happened? Identify what has grown — if anything!

Grow some vegetable tops — try carrots, turnips, beetroot. Place tops on a saucer of gravel and water and leave. Place in a warm sunny position. Leaves should appear after a week or so. Draw graphs to illustrate growth rates. Keep a photographic record.   •

Try collecting some seeds from wild flowers you have successfully grown and plant them out. Perhaps one of the parents has a suitable garden spot, or there may be a corner of a field or wild area in the school grounds. Be sure to get permission from the landowner and expert advice before any seeds are sown in a "wild" location.

Conservation may not be served if a strong species is introduced which takes over the habitat of a rare but delicate wild flower! In general, the advice is **not** to introduce wildflower seeds into a natural area.

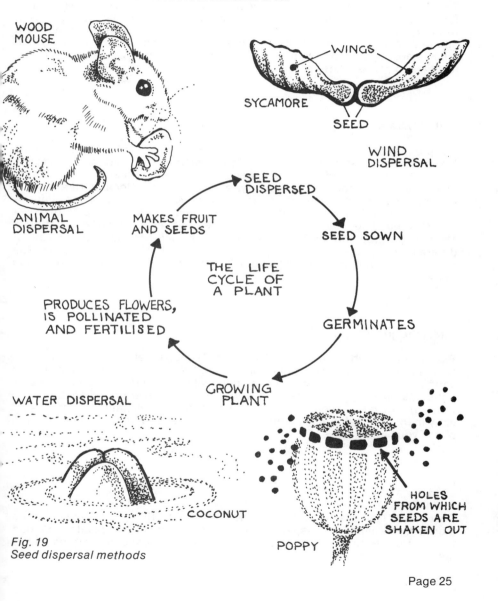

WOOD MOUSE

ANIMAL DISPERSAL

WINGS

SYCAMORE

SEED

WIND DISPERSAL

SEED DISPERSED

MAKES FRUIT AND SEEDS

SEED SOWN

THE LIFE CYCLE OF A PLANT

PRODUCES FLOWERS, IS POLLINATED AND FERTILISED

GERMINATES

GROWING PLANT

WATER DISPERSAL

COCONUT

POPPY

HOLES FROM WHICH SEEDS ARE SHAKEN OUT

Fig. 19
Seed dispersal methods

9
Extension Ideas for TOPIC WORK — Themes in Brief

Topic ideas can be developed alongside the investigative work. Whether to follow-up or what to follow-up will be a decision for the teacher. Some areas of work will be more applicable than others and in any case the needs and interests of the children will influence the direction taken. The following themes are suggested in note form and will hopefully provide a few ideas for teachers to use as 'starters'.

Soil, rocks and stones

The process of erosion, weathering of rocks. Frost, ice, wind and water factors. Decaying plant matter. What is soil? Soil erosion — the need for a vegetation cover. Simple work on rocks — igneous, sedimentary, metamorphic. Earthquakes and volcanoes. Visit a quarry, a stonemason, a local natural history museum. Experiment with different materials, eg. stone, brick, tiles, slate — devise tests for porosity, hardness. Explore the neighbourhood to discover different building materials and their uses. Observe shape and patterns. Measuring, graphing and classification possibilities. Make a display of different rocks, fossils, building materials. The Parable of the Sower. The House Built on Rock/Sand (Matthew 7. 24). The Building Song (Come and Praise, BBC).

Under the ground

Pipes, drains, cables, mains and tunnels. The Channel Tunnel. The London Underground. People who work underground eg. miners. Things made from earth's materials eg. pottery, building materials, oil and its by-products. Visit a pottery, a building site, some road works. Animals underground eg. the mole, the worm. Caves — their formation, stalactites and stalagmites — homes for early man. Cave paintings. Paintings using natural resources. Make dyes from plants you have grown.

Land use study

Do a simple land use study. This will get the children thinking about the soil as a growing medium — trees, arable and pastoral farming use, plants. The food we eat. Uses of timber. Visit a local farm. If no local farms then arrange a trip out into the countryside to see one.

Starting a School Garden *Topic Work*

Plant study

The different parts of a plant and their functions eq. roots, stems, leaves, flowers. What conditions are necessary for successful growth — germination. The life cycle of a flower. Seed dispersal. The parts of plants we eat. The economic importance of some plants. Leaves make food — take a look at photosynthesis. Annuals, biennials, perennials. Plants that eat insects eg. sundew, the venus flytrap, bladderwort. Poisonous plants eg. laburnum, deadly nightshade, foxgloves. Unusual plants eg. baobab trees, stone plants, giant water lilies. Flowers as symbols eg. the poppy — Remembrance Day, daffodils and leeks as Welsh emblems, the shamrock of Ireland, the thistle of Scotland, the wars of the Roses.

Discuss and make graphs of favourite flowers, fruits, vegetables. Sorting tasks eg. into colours, into fruit or vegetable, into evergreen or deciduous. Visit the local grocer/fruiterer. List the vegetables and fruit on sale. Classify as home grown or imported, sweet fruits or bitter fruits, root crops or other types. Choose a particular fruit or vegetable and find out how and where it is grown. Make a world fruit survey.

Fig. 20
Make a fruit survey

Collect and learn some songs about flowers.

Plants of the Bible eg. trees . . . *fig, palm, olive, vine.* Flowers — *lily, anemone. Wheat and tares. Flax, papyrus, reeds* and *rushes.*

Plant habitats — make a comparative study of some general plant habitats, eg. deserts, wetlands, mountain areas. Discover how plants adapt to their particular environmental situation.

Seeds

Collect different seeds of flowers, fruits, trees and grass. Study similarities and differences. Get inside a seed, get inside a fruit. What do you find? Food store, embryo. How does a seed grow? Germination — needs moisture, warmth and air. Make some simple musical instruments using seeds and yoghurt pots, margarine tubs and small tins. Paint and decorate them.

Cultivation

The history of cultivation. New Stone Age times. Crop rotation, medieval strip farming. Hand tools give way to mechanisation, horses and oxen to tractors. Arable and pastoral farming. Harvest ideas — and festivals. Land reclamation. The history of garden tools — prehistoric to present day. Make a display of present day tools. Visit a museum of local history — perhaps you can loan a collection of bygone tools.

Famous Gardens — the Garden of Eden, Garden of Gethsemane, Hanging Gardens of Babylon. Garden designs of famous houses and stately homes. Formal and informal layouts. Topiary. Bottle garden. Cacti garden.

Garden creatures

Make a study of one or more creatures eg. earthworm, centipede, millipede, slugs, ladybird, greenfly, aphid, butterfly, bee, birds. How do creatures help or hinder the gardener? How do insects help flowers? What attracts them — consider size, shape, position, height, scent and colour? Study the parts of a flower — stamen, pistil, ovule, sepals, carpels. Pollination and fertilisation. How can we control garden pests? Discuss the use of insecticides. Make a vivarium and/or a wormery. Discover how creatures depend on each other for survival. Graphs — number of creatures seen, favourite birds. Can you identify the tracks made by certain creatures? Look in the snow, in the mud or put out an area of sand.

Make and use bird nesting boxes and a bird table. Develop a window **hide** (cover a window with sugar paper and leave a viewing strip) so children may observe the bird table. Record food preferences and bird behaviour.

Experimental Packs — from School Garden Company

Several different packs are available. Each gives much more detailed information on practical investigations and topic work for teachers and children with a particular type and range of plants. Included in each pack are seeds (sufficient for the whole class), information booklet for the teacher, and work sheets for children (which may be photocopied). More details of these useful aids can be found in the catalogue of the School Garden Company — see **Appendix** for address.

Further ideas

Social — look at the **Country Code** — respect and concern for all the countryside.

Moral — plan a **school assembly** about your school garden. Show the whole school what you are doing. Get them interested. Perhaps some others will want to share the project.

Art/design/craft — seed mosaics, seed collage, paper flowers, leaf rubbings, textile work, observational drawings using pencil, pens, ink, pastels. Look at shape, colour, texture, pattern. Clay modelling, photography. Make a collection of pressed flowers. Dried flowers.

Music/movement — musical instruments made from seeds and plastic pots or tins. Creative music making eg. plants opening and closing, sun and rain on growing plants. Movement work eg. growth, wilting in the sun, the different movements of the garden creatures, farm machinery, eg. combines, threshing machines. Pair and group work.

Mathematics — scale work, mapping out plots. Use a base line and sighting points, simple surveying. Area, perimeter, costing quantities, percentages, eg. of germination rates. Keeping of weather records, eg. wind direction recorded on a wind rose, rain gauges, maximum/minimum thermometers.

Language — discussion, recording, using reference materials. Story writing, poetry writing. Descriptive work.

Resources

The following items represent a selection only of items which you may find useful for your school garden and the school work which comes from it.

A. Useful practical equipment

Most garden centres sell a selection of tools. However, take care that the **size** (and quality/price) will be suitable for your children. Many of the tools are available (in suitably-sized versions) from the **School Garden Company** — see their catalogue.

Fork	Flower pots (assorted sizes)
Spade	Broom
Trowels	Wooden or plastic labels
Hoe	Soil test kit
Rake	Electronic thermometer
Dibber	Seed trays
Watering can	Camera
Polythene bags	Tape measure
Garden line	Pooters
Magnifying glasses	Yoghurt pots
Measuring equipment	Paving stones
Sand	Compost/manure

B. Books — a selection of helpful books for teachers and children

Reference

Science 5-13 Project (series for teachers)	Macdonald
... particularly **Minibeasts** 0-356-04106-9	Macdonald
Using the Environment (set of 6 titles) 0-356-05364-4	Macdonald
(also in Science 5-13 project for teachers)	
Project Environment — Schools Council	Longman
Nature Trail Series	Usborne
Young Scientist Investigates Series	Oxford U.P.
Young Explorer Series	Wayland
The Soil — Helen Piers	Angus and Robertson
Botany — Ladybird Science Series	Ladybird
Plants of the Bible — Little Lion	Lion Publishing
Wild Flowers of Britain	Book Club Associates
Wild Flowers	Octopus
Observer Book Series (selected titles)	Warne
Do You Know How Plants Grow?	Piccolo
Growing Trees — Irene Finch 0-582-18163-1	Longman
Close-up on Nature (series) Swallow & Soothill	Longman
Life Cycle Books (series for ages 5-7) - Althea	Longman
Growing Things - Anna Pavard 0-333-30858-1	Macmillan

William Curtis Easy-to-Find Field Guides
  (set of 4 titles) 0-435-04554-7   Heinemann

Childrens' Fiction

Tom's Midnight Garden   Oxford U.P.
The Secret Garden   Puffin
The Bongleweed   Puffin
Under the Autumn Garden   Kestrel
Johnny Appleseed (short story)

Poetry

In the street of the fruit stalls/Digging from Preludes   Heinemann
The burning of the leaves/The Creation from Six
  Anthologies (2)   Ginn
The mole/Hannibal the Snail/The golden boy from
  Third Poetry Book   Oxford U.P.
The barn/Transplanting from Full Swing   Evans
The snail/The green spring from Fancy Free   Evans
Here we come a-haying from Going Out   Evans
Tall nettles/Seed shop from Patterns of Poetry   Burke

C. Wallcharts/Slides

Countryside Charts   Macmillan Education
Posters: Small Creatures, The Country Code,
        Hedgerows, Underground   Philip Green
Photographs/Poem sets (various)   Philip Green
Soils and Rocks — Radiovision   BBC Publications
Slides/film strips: Hedgerows, Underground
  (and others)   Philip Green
The life of a Hedge/The life of a Wasteland   Slide Centre, Ilton,
  (slides)   Somerset TA19 9HS
Nature in the Garden — slide set   Slide Centre

D. Music

Waltz of the Flowers — Nutcracker Suite   Tchaikovsky
English Country Garden
John Barleycorn
The Floral Dance   trad. Cornish tune
The Garden Song   John Denver
Bird Song recordings (various)   RSPB

E. Computer Software

First Filer — Chalksoft Ltd., P.O. Box 49, Spalding, Lincs.
A database for children 6—10 + . Very easy to use. Children can build their own databases of (for example) insects, wild flowers. The base can then be searched for "sets" of many types according to the investigation in progress.
Leaves/Pond Animals — Heinemann/SMDP
Two programmes which allow children (10 +) to identify specimens by answering the computer's questions.

F. Useful addresses — suppliers and interest groups.

School Garden Company — suppliers of wild flower and grass seeds. Also various experimental packs on plants (complete with seeds) and equipment and accessories for school gardens.
P.O. Box 49, Spalding, Lincs. PE11 1NZ.   0775-69518

Council for Environmental Education (regular newsletter/reviews)
School of Education, University of Reading, Reading, RG1 5AQ.

National Association for Environmental Education
73 Hazelwood Road, Adcocks Green, Birmingham B27.

The Urban Wildlife Unit (conservation group)
C/o Landlife, The Old Police Station, Lark Lane, Liverpool, L17 8UU.

The Countryside Commission
John Dower House, Crescent Place, Cheltenham, Gloucestershire, GL50 3RA.

Greenpeace (conservation group)
36 Graham Street, London, N18 8LL.

Friends of the Earth Ltd. (conservation group)
377 City Road, London, EC1V 1NA.

The School Natural Science Society
C/o Association for Science Education, College Lane, Hatfield, Herts.

Royal Society for Protection of Birds (RSPB)
The Lodge, Sandy, Beds.

Science Equipment News/CLEAPSE (regular teacher news sheet)
School Science Service, Brunel University, Uxbridge, UB8 3PH.

Fig. 21
In your garden . . . .